To Clare Ansberry, in appreciation and respect for your (and your colleagues') journalistic integrity which keeps business on their toes.

Phillip Hartley Smith

Winter 2002

QUAKER BUSINESS ETHICS

QUAKER BUSINESS ETHICS

A Plumb Line Guide to Practical Applications

in

Business and Industry

Business Ethics from a Quaker Point of View

The American Quaker Business Consortium

Phillip Hartley Smith, editor

2001

This edition published by Diamond Library Publishers, a division of Diamond Analytics Corporation, by arrangements with Phillip Hartley Smith, the American Quaker Business Consortium, and Benjamin Rowntree, the Quakers and Business Group.

Diamond Library Publishers
15 Cannon Road
Wilton, CT 06897

Telephone 203-834-1231

Cover design by Stephen Wade Lunsford

First edition: October, 2001

Printed in the United States of America

ISBN 1-880-876-76-0

Library of Congress cataloging-in information:

Smith, Phillip Hartley
Quaker Business Ethics (title)
      1. Business ethics, Christian, Quaker
      2. Religious Society of Friends, Business ethics
      3. Christian ethics
HF 5387
BX7733.B8 2001

"This is what the Lord showed me: the Lord was standing beside a wall built with a plumb line, with a plumb line in his hand. And the Lord said to me, "Amos, what do you see?" And I said, "A plumb line." Then the Lord said, "See, I am setting a plumb line in the midst of my people …"

- Amos 7:7-8

"The object of business is to make money in an honorable manner. The object of life is to do good."

- Peter Cooper

Acknowledgments

Thanks are due to a number of people without whose efforts this small text could not have been completed. First, to the English Friends, Ben Rowntree and Susan Montgomery and colleagues, who began this work. In Australia, I want to thank Sir Arvi Parbo, retired Chairman of the BHP Company and Alcoa Australia; Templeton Prize Winner Dr. Charles Birch; and Dr. Simon Longstaff of the St. James Ethics Center. In the United States, I want to express my gratitude to Dean Alan White of M.I.T.'s Sloan School; environmental scientist Dr. Dale Keairns; Father George Lundy, S.J., PhD, President of Wheeling Jesuit University; Father Paul Jesuraja, S.J. PhD of the same university; Jay Marshall, Dean of the Earlham School of Religion; and John Chapman Benson, a Friend who is a friend indeed. And, finally, to Martha Dittrich Smith, my dear and faithful friend of forty eight years, for her insights and encouragement; she keeps my compass card adjusted to True North, for which I am truly grateful. And, in appreciation to all who read and commented so helpfully, thank you.

In closing, any errors or omissions are all mine, so please do not hesitate to let me know when and where you see them.

Phillip Hartley Smith
Fox Chapel, Pennsylvania
Autumn, 2001

Contents

Working With People

The Community

Unethical Business Practices

Vision, Practice, and Pragmatism

Advice from an American Quaker Businessman

Quaker Methods For Decision Making

Preface

Advices and Queries are fundamental to the life of members of the Religious Society of Friends, also known as Quakers. The use of Advices began in England in 1656, instituted by the Elders at Balby. Revisions were made in 1682 and further expanded in 1694. By 1723, the term "Advices and Queries" was in general use, and additions continued throughout the next two centuries. Changes came through a careful process of inspiration, proposal, discussion, discernment and acceptance in the Quaker traditional practice of arriving at "Sense of the Meeting."

Further revisions took place in the twentieth century, by which time these ideas were collected and presented as both Advices and Queries, intended as guidelines for Quakers' personal and corporate lives. While there are some differences in the Advices and Queries one would see between say, those published by U.K. Quakers, Australian, Canadian, and American, for example, the underlying core would be similar.

The Advices and Queries are, in fact, the faith and practice guide for Quakers, read daily in personal devotions and read weekly in the local Friends' meetings. It is from this history that a reader will understand this attempt to set out the practical application of Quaker faith and practice in a similar format for business and industry in this new millennium.

"Dearly beloved Friends, these things we do not lay upon you as a rule or form to walk by, but that all, with a measure of light which is pure and holy, may be guided: and so in the light walking and abiding, these things may be fulfilled in the Spirit, not in the letter -- *for the letter killeth, but the Spirit giveth life.*"

- This postscript, ending with a quotation from Second Corinthians 3:6, was included in an epistle of Advices from the Elders at Balby, Yorkshire, England, 1656, writing to the fledgling meetings in the north of England.

INTRODUCTION

William Penn, an early Quaker, said, "True godliness does not turn men out of the world but enables them to live better in it and excites their endeavors to mend it." Quakers believe that, as we grow in awareness of God's will for our lives, we begin to translate our experience of the Holy into active life. Hence, we have always emphasized integrity in personal conduct and service in the betterment of the world and its people as an integral part of the spiritual life. Many Quaker businesses have been recognized as forerunners in fair dealing, good business practice, and care for employees.

For over two centuries Quakers have used booklets entitled "Advices and Queries" as a challenge and inspiration in their personal lives. Those Advices and Queries are not rules or requirements; rather they represent ideals to aspire to and standards of excellence to strive for. They provide guidance for us in our personal and corporate conduct. It is in this spirit that we offer these Advices and Queries for people in business, industry, and nonprofit entities.

This book is addressed to anyone working in any kind of enterprise who is concerned with ethics in business. It has been published first by English and later by American Quakers, all of whom have worked, or are working, in a variety of businesses run with the intention of making a profit. We believe that we should live our lives in accordance with our beliefs. We try to do so, and we believe our work in business and our spiritual lives to be compatible.

Not everyone shares our view. Today, many people, Quakers and others, are so dismayed at the unethical business practices they see around them, that some have come to believe that business itself is unethical. Some Quakers question whether the world of business is compatible with our testimonies on social justice, equality, peace and the environment. Others wonder whether a system, which utilizes different levels of rewards for effort, is consistent with our most fundamental belief in respecting that of God in everyone. Some wonder if the term "ethical business" is not in itself oxymoronic. We respect their concerns. We respect similar concerns of those in other Christian denominations and also the concerns of those in other faith traditions. Yet we remain sure of our conviction.

The world of work is an imperfect one. We know as authors that we have not lived up to all the advice offered, and could not honestly answer every query in this book in the ideal. We recognize that this is part of being human. We recognize that some business activities are inappropriate. We acknowledge that there can be an "unacceptable face of capitalism," and we also know that the opposite is at work too! Nonetheless, we are called to live in the world while not needing to be of the world. We believe that through the interaction of our faith and our ability in business we can help provide those resources we all need to live our lives.

These Advices and Queries cannot cover every business circumstance. Yet our faith is an experimental one and also, traditionally, an adventurous one. These offerings are our interpretations of the world of work as we see it, and the questions we might ask of ourselves. We offer them in that spirit so that they might assist others when faced with a problem requiring resolution. Resolving problems is both the art and science of management. Remember the ends for your action, as well as the means. If that objective is important and consistent with your faith, then the action will be worthwhile, and appropriate means must be found. If it is not, then restraint or further consideration is required. This, we believe, is faith in action in the workplace, whether that be the home, office, shop, field or factory, for wherever people are at work, there is that of God within them.

The principal authors of the seminal text are members of a British Quaker business group, who acknowledge and express their gratitude to the many contributions and support which have come from the conference on Business and Ethics run by Woodbrooke Quaker Study Center, Birmingham, UK, in June 2000, and many other people in the UK and the USA. Lead members of the English Friends group were Ben Rowntree, Susan Rowntree, Roland Carn, and Richard Murphy. The American Quaker Business Consortium is indeed grateful for the leadership they have provided with this text and their kind grant of permission for us to reproduce it in an American context in the United States.

QUAKER TESTIMONIES

Four basic testimonies have sprung from our faith and have guided us over the years. They are not imposed or required of Friends, but are part of our distinctive witness. We start with these four fundamental testimonies, which we believe apply to all our lives, and interpret them in a business context.

1. Honesty and Integrity

Advice

The most important word to remember in all business dealings is integrity. Integrity is essential to developing trust. We know that a person is acting with integrity when he or she is not moved by opportunistic or self-seeking motives; thus we can trust their performance in any business situation.

Integrity requires being transparent, honest, truthful and consistent with your beliefs in all business dealings. The core structure of business requires trust, faith, and goodwill. With the rapid growth of the global and digital economy, establishing and maintaining trust is a critical factor for success.

Queries

Are you honest and truthful in all that you say and do?

If pressure is brought upon you to lower your standard of integrity, are you prepared to resist such pressures?

Do you do what you promise to do, even if it is just to return a phone call?

2. Simplicity

Advice

Often, the most happy and serene people live a simple life. By contrast, stress, overwork, and insecurity can be prevalent in high-pressure business situations, increasingly so in the so-called global economy. In business, as in our personal lives, we can be consumed by our own desire for more, as well as by the demands of others.

The practice of simplicity helps us to eliminate all that is superfluous, and to put first things first. This requires strong principles, focused vision, sensitive understanding, clear communication, and management actions which are predictable, firm, appropriate, and timely.

Queries

Do you make time to review your priorities in the light of your clearest and best thinking?

When faced with conflicting demands, do you weigh them carefully in the light of your priorities and endeavor to put the more important things first?

Do you scrutinize your desires and consider how you might simplify your needs?

Are you easily persuaded to buy something you do not need or cannot afford?

Is there real need for lavish business entertainment or luxurious office space?

Can you achieve the same business end result in a modest yet functional way?

3. Equality

Advice

When we can accept that every person has "that of God" within, we can then acknowledge that every one of us is equal before our Creator God; we treasure that in our Constitution and can do no less than practice that in our work. Be alert to practices both here and throughout the world that discriminate against people on the basis of who or what they are or because of their race, gender, color, creed, or national origin.

Queries

Do you respect and encourage diversity as a source of energy and strength in your business?

Do you refrain from making prejudiced judgments or statements about others?

Do you see to it that others do likewise?

When recruiting, evaluating, or promoting employees, are you careful not to differentiate among candidates on the grounds of age, sex, color, religion, national origin, or any other characteristic that is not related to job performance?

If an employee has a disability, do you try to find work that they can do effectively?

Do you make alterations in your working methods and workplace to accommodate special needs?

Do you help all to overcome their special challenges?

4. Peace

Advice

Conflict occurs, and will continue to occur, even in the most peaceful of worlds; regrettably it is a part of human nature. In business, as in the rest of life, how we deal with our own anger and how we find peaceful solutions to conflict are important. What matters most, however, is to work towards creating a culture of peaceful resolution of conflict, thus reducing and eliminating the potential for confrontational hostility at all levels: personal, business, national, international -- and the human costs resulting from such strife. This also requires searching out anything in our conduct of business that might contain the seeds of war or otherwise damage or threaten life.

Quakers believe that there is "that of God" in everyone. This leads to one of the most strongly held beliefs: that it is wrong to kill anyone and therefore all forms of war are wrong. Conflict should be preempted through active peacekeeping and, when it does flare up, should be resolved while preserving respect for all concerned. Avoid doing any business which promotes warfare in any form.

Queries

When you disagree with a colleague, customer, or supplier, are you willing to consider that you may be the one who is mistaken?

Are you willing to give others the benefit of the doubt?

When you are angry, do you act in an inappropriate way? Are you able to control anger and, if necessary, express your anger in a way that results in finding a solution and thereby creating a positive effect from a negative cause?

What is your basic focus in managing the business?

Do you believe that success is achieved primarily by beating the competition at any cost?

Does your company earn any income from products or processes that unnecessarily threaten and/or degrade human life?

Do you audit your product mix from time to time to evaluate these considerations?

CONDUCT OF BUSINESS

When we really face up to the fact that everything we have comes to us as a gift from God, we come to understand that we are all stewards accountable for our use of time, people, money, and natural resources. In each situation a good steward seeks the right balance between prudence and adventure, conservatism and creation, leading and serving, stimulating and supporting.

Good business is the way we serve the social and economic community, whether individually or corporately, in national or international organizations. Its principles apply equally to commercial entities, charities and not-for-profit enterprises, non-governmental groups, and last, but not least, to government, because all are to be managed at such a standard of excellence as to optimize success, since, in all of these, moneys other than our own personal wealth are at risk.

5. Business and Profit

Advice

It is not unethical to make a profit. In fact, the reverse is true; no business will survive for long without profits. What matters is how you make profits and what is done with those profits.

In order to maintain and to increase employment, it is necessary to be profitable and to build resources for the future. Profit is needed for human, facilities, and product and process development, and for appropriate public service support to the communities in which you operate. Your employees deserve the security of knowing they are working for a prudently managed company that is profitable rather than the insecurity of working for a money-losing business.

As a manager, always remember that you are a trustee. Your shareholders may be individuals, pension funds, charitable endowments, and your employees. All of these constituencies are "the trusters" who are trusting you to manage well. When using moneys in your business, other than your own personal wealth, you have an obligation to preserve the capital employed and earn the maximum return on that capital consistent with the highest standards implied in the spirit and intent of the governing secular laws and your faith-based ethics.

Queries

Are the purposes of your business clear to all of your stakeholders, meaning everyone who has an interest in the success of your enterprise: employees and retirees, customers and suppliers, community and government, shareholders and other investors?

Are all activities focused on achieving these objectives?

What is the driving force of your business? Is it only to maximize profits, or is it to provide for the interests of *all* stakeholders?

Are you maintaining your facilities and workplaces to best available technology (as needed) and state of the art condition?

Are you managing in such a way as to provide sustainable employment for your people? Do you build your employees' confidence, skills and self-worth? Do you provide products and services that contribute to the well-being of the whole society in which you enjoy the privilege of operating?

After paying to your shareholders a fair and equitable return on their investment, are your retained earnings sufficient to sustain and grow your business into a secure future?

Are your profits earned in an ethical and legal way?

If you have little-to-no competition, do you make excessive profits? In the conduct of your business, do you provide good quality at a fair price? Are you tempted to raise your prices and make a bigger profit just because the market will bear it at certain times?

6. Uncertainty and Risk

Advice

Uncertainty and risk are inherent in every business. There is uncertainty because we do not always have available complete information on the present business climate, its future trends, and the full end-result of prior business plans.

Develop prudent management plans for contingencies and sound risk management so as not to jeopardize the interests of the stakeholders of your business. Remember the "reasonably prudent man rule" and also the proverb, "He who manages only by his crystal ball should learn to eat ground glass."

Queries

Do you routinely review your business risks and seek competent advice and counsel on how to manage them?

Do you take all appropriate steps to eliminate unnecessary business risks?

Do you make sure that people affected by a risk know about it?

Do you seek to contain and limit the consequences of risk, through appropriate insurance?

Do you have contingency plans ready to deal with unexpected events?

Do you avoid excessive risks so as not to harm the best interests of all your stakeholders, particularly your employees, and not put the future of your business in jeopardy?

7. Responsibilities of Directors and Managers

Advice

Directors and managers have the primary responsibility to consider carefully all of the stakeholders in the business: investors, customers, suppliers, employees, retirees, communities, and governmental agencies.

A business must comply with the spirit and intent of all applicable laws and regulations. If you consider a law or regulation to be at variance with either your own social and ethical testimonies or prudent business practice, seek counsel before taking action, and consider working to change the law.

Always strive to utilize such management practices as to create an atmosphere and culture in your workplace that is conducive to high productivity, good health and safety (both physical and mental). Aim to create a work-success satisfaction so that all concerned feel it was earned with integrity and dignity.

Queries

Do you keep fully informed of your legal and fiduciary responsibilities as a director and/or manager?

Do you take timely and proactive actions and steps to discharge those responsibilities and keep clear, accurate, and complete records when deemed both prudent and necessary?

Do you regularly audit the company's managerial competence and the social and moral health of your business?

Do you set, communicate, and maintain ethical standards of business conduct? Have you established monitoring systems for faithful compliance and reporting in these areas?

If your organization is found to be operating in a way you believe to be unethical, do you carefully consider what part you or another must play, either to correct or to remedy the situation?

Do you make sure that your shareholders receive all the information that they need to value their investment fully and accurately, in clear and concise language that all can understand?

8. Obligations to Shareholders and Investors

Advice

A growth company will always have a need for retained earnings and increased capital from new investors to take advantage of any and all opportunities for growth, and for holding and gaining market share. Shareholders provide that necessary capital and must be compensated by dividends and/or share price appreciation.

Small shareholders may appear to have a small voice in the company, but their concerns should be heard and considered, or your reputation as a business may suffer. Remember that any shareholder can "vote with their feet" at any time, simply by placing a sell order with their broker. Their concerns should be heard and treated with respect, or the company's standing as a business will eventually suffer.

Queries

Does your management performance provide your shareholders a fair return on their investment without putting their capital at undue risk?

Are you managing for long-term appreciation of their investment?

Do you cut corners on prudent maintenance and capital expenditures in order to dress up the bottom line or inflate apparent return on shareholders' investment?

Do your communications with your shareholders give all necessary information about the progress of the company in clear, concise, and understandable ways?

Are you following Generally Accepted Accounting Principles (GAAP) in your financial accounting and reporting?

Does the board have a fully independent audit committee that follows best practices for such committees as recommended by the American Institute of Certified Public Accountants and the Financial Accounting Standards Board?

9. Ethical Business Practices

Advice

Wages should reflect the contribution each worker makes to her or his company. Wages and work requirements should enable them to meet their own needs and those of their dependents, and to contribute to their sustainable family growth and those of their community. Very low pay can well be regarded as a modern form of slavery.

Queries

Does your company invest in, conduct business with, buy from, use as a tax haven, or launder money in any country in which there are egregious and ongoing violations of human rights?

Does your company use or contract with companies that rely on the labor of children who are thus prevented from obtaining a basic education because of their work? Does your company contract with companies that do not pay their employees a sustainable living wage in their own communities?

In collective bargaining negotiations, do you overtly or subtly threaten to move your operations to lower-cost regions or third-world countries in order to wring concessions from your employees?

10. Environmental Responsibilities

Advice

In recent decades, businessmen and women have learned that we have a fundamental responsibility to operate our businesses both at home and abroad in such a way so as not to damage the physical, chemical, and economic environments in which we operate. This is a worldwide responsibility, whether we like it or not.

We cannot any longer just consider the impact our business has on our immediate environment. In reality, the environment is a silent stakeholder in the business. Make sure you do not cause health and quality of life problems not only to your employees, but also to your neighbors in your plant communities, by excessive noise, fumes, smoke, questionable fluids effluent, accumulation of unsightly waste, or by poor housekeeping at your plant facilities and environs.

Queries

Do you routinely evaluate your products, processes and services to be sure you are discharging your responsibilities with integrity towards maintaining a sustainable world environment? Do you then, if necessary, seek out and implement best practices to improve operations under your control?

If you have an environmental problem, do you correct it, or merely move it to some other location or country where standards and their enforcement are easier?

Do you maintain a recycling program and use recycled products where possible?

Do you provide a product or service that is in any way harmful to health? If so, are there clear warnings?

Do you have a monitored environmental policy and report annually on your progress?

11. Health, Safety, and Security

Advice

All employers and employees have a duty to make sure their working practices and equipment are safe for all users and the general public. They should also exercise prudent security and take steps to minimize risks to the health, safety and welfare of others, including their employees, customers or anyone affected by the products or services supplied.

Queries

Do you take all reasonable and appropriate steps to comply with health and safety regulations?

Do you tolerate compromises on safety practices in order to reduce costs?

Do you work with others to ensure that best practices, standards, regulations and legislation are developed to promote the public good?

When you observe a product or practice that poses a hazard, do you report it?

If a hazardous situation arises in your business, do you take immediate steps to correct the situation?

12. Quality and Safety of Products and Services

Advice

Quakers have a long-standing reputation for providing good quality at a fair price. This reputation enhanced their businesses. There is ample evidence in business writings to show that this is good business practice and pays its own dividends.

At an absolute minimum, suppliers have a fundamental responsibility to ensure that the products and/or services they sell will not cause foreseeable physical or financial damage to their customers.

Queries

Do you continually strive to improve the quality and safety of your products?

Do you have a quality assurance and control-reporting program that is independent of the manufacturing management?

Does your product have an intentionally built-in obsolescence, in order that the customer will have to replace it sooner than the customer thought appropriate?

Do your products and services comply with the law and other regulations?

Are your products and services safe, fit for use, suitable for their purpose, appropriately designed and produced on a sustainable continuing basis?

Have your products been carefully and independently assessed for any possible damage or loss they could cause to customers or others?

Have you provided adequate warnings of any dangers?

Have you both ensured and insured such that others can be made whole in the event your product causes unforeseen harm or dissatisfaction?

13. Advertising and Promotion

Advice

Advertising and promotional activities are a real test of our commitment to honesty and integrity in business. Consider carefully your advertising program, both for what your advertisements say, or omit to say, and where you advertise.

Queries

In your advertisements, are you careful to avoid misleading statements and claims?

Do you make sure that your product and service claims

and promises are justified and realistic?

Does your advertising present a true and accurate picture of your products and services?

Are you selling goods and services of real value or are you selling image?

Are your advertising placements and media selected with ethical care?

Are you aiming your advertising inappropriately at particularly vulnerable markets, such as children, or "credit-holics" susceptible to impulse buying on credit with little or no hope of repayment? Is your advertising budget appropriate to the desired end result?

Are the promotional costs an appropriate proportion of the final price?

MONEY MATTERS

Money has been, is, and will continue to be a complex commodity. Our use of money has the power to do either good or evil. It should be remembered that money has powerful symbolic and psychological connotations and implications that can lead people to behave in unexpected ways. In business, money and its use are merely resources to achieve your business objectives. Making more money should not become an obsessive goal in itself.

14. Investments

Advice

Think and act carefully on how you invest surplus funds not immediately needed as working capital in the revenue cycle. Invest these funds prudently so that they are immediately available at no risk when needed once again in the business.

Seek to invest in activities or enterprises that add to the local or global economy, and that will be a positive factor in improving the quality of life and standard of living.

Consider all the conditions under which the income is produced and the total effects the investments have on the welfare of all concerned.

Queries

Does your company invest in, or earn revenue from, activities that may be considered unethical or harmful to life? These may include alcohol, drugs, tobacco, firearms, military weapons and supplies, and gambling.

Do you utilize the company's retained earnings effectively for the shareholders' optimum total return? Do you consider proportional payouts, allowing owners of the capital to re-invest elsewhere? Do you use money entrusted to you with prudence, discretion and responsibility? When you lend money, is the loan properly recorded and secured? Is the interest rate fair and appropriate for the risk involved?

15. Prompt Payment

Advice

In managing your accounts payable, remember that payment is owed when materials are received against a valid purchase order or a task is completed. Many small businesses experience serious cash flow problems and may even face bankruptcy because of insufficient cash flow to pay their own bills and not because of poor management. Often this is because other and often larger companies with more commercial clout, choose not to pay promptly, in effect forcing their suppliers to finance their revenue cycle. Make sure you pay your bills on a fair and timely schedule.

Queries

Do you know and honor your suppliers' terms?

Do you delay payment at the expense of your supplier?

Do you make your own terms clear, and do you deal fairly, firmly, and consistently with those who do not honor them?

16. Financial Accounting

Advice

The company's financial statements are important records of your business. Accordingly, they must accurately state your financial position in clear and understandable terms. The information they contain should be appropriately available to those publishing credit ratings, your bankers and other lenders, so that all who do business with you can clearly understand the financial health of their customer or supplier. Unless you keep careful financials and review them on a timely basis, you will be running the risk of not managing the business to its optimum success level. This is unacceptable fiduciary stewardship to the multiple constituencies who have placed their trust in your management.

Do not rely just on historic financial data. It is always important to develop and utilize predictive accounting control systems so that you can manage for a pre-planned performance end result.

Make certain that those entrusted with the handling of company funds are fully competent to do so, bonded, and trustworthy. Practice segregation of duties to avoid any unnecessary presence of undue temptation.

Queries

Do you make sure the company's financial records are true and accurate in all respects, and follow GAAP?

Are your monthly, quarterly, and annual financials prepared on a timely basis and promptly communicated to all who need prompt feedback for optimum management performance?

Do you audit your accounting systems to ensure that the control mechanisms are adequate?

Are you vigilant against fraud, honest mistakes and malicious deceit?

Do you provide financial reports to all who need to know on a timely basis: shareholders, lenders, and credit rating agencies? Do you include all your employees, with information in an understandable form?

17. Taxes

Advice

Avoiding the payment of excess tax by organizing your financial affairs so that neither you nor your company has to pay more tax than the law requires is simply good management. Evading tax by financial manipulation and reporting thereof in order to escape paying taxes that are legally due is a form of theft. It is important to consider carefully the line separating these two, since not all professional advisors are clear on the distinction between the two, especially when they see potential and attractive fee income for a looser shading of the distinction.

Queries

When a way of avoiding or minimizing tax is suggested, do you consider carefully whether it is an appropriate practice and not an evasion?

In your management of the business, is tax planning sometimes an overly important driver of your business plan?

Do you deal honestly with the tax authorities?

Do you view the payment of accurately computed taxes as a duty of your business to society?

Do you make sure that your accounting records are complete and accurate, and that there is no question that your tax returns meet the required standards of the tax authorities?

18. Remuneration

Advice

Remuneration is not only salary and wages; it also includes hospitalization and medical benefits, bonuses, pension contributions, stock options, tuition reimbursement for continuing education, travel accident and life insurance, subsidized cafeterias, company cars, social security payments, and day care for children of working parents. It is a return for work well done and good management practice.

Wage and salary ranges reflect market forces, and the current high, and in many cases, obscene salary packages for some top officers may indeed reflect a shortage of competent key executives. However, excessive remuneration and abuse of perquisites by management will cause envy and resentment that are corrosive both within the company and society at large.

Compensation differences in an organization must be logical and well understood by all concerned.

Queries

If you get a large compensation package, do you make sure the same reward principles apply to all others in your organization?

In order to maintain both a real and perceived sense of equity in your organization, do you see to it that a reasonable ratio of the highest compensation package to the lowest is maintained?

If your compensation is linked to profit, or return on shareholders' investment, do you achieve this end by downsizing, layoffs, or moving plants to regions and countries with lower labor costs?

Do you make sure that your wage and salary packages are such that employees do not need to depend on second jobs, excessive overtime or other means that may damage the quality of their family life in order to supplement their pay?

Is it your standard management tactic to pay just the cheapest wage and salary packages you can get away with?

Do you ensure that part-time workers have access to the same benefits as full-time, if only on a proportionate scale? Do you seek to use zero-benefits part-time help as a dodge to keep your fringe benefit costs down?

Do you provide adequate pension benefits to all your employees?

Are benefits fully portable, including company contributions, should the employee leave your company?

Are the pension benefits for top management unreasonably "sweeter" than those for other employees, and are they fully disclosed for all to see?

If you require your employees to work overtime, do you compensate them appropriately?

Do you use mandatory overtime as a way of avoiding hiring additional full-time employees?

When your employees live in company housing as part of their job location, is provision made by either the employee and/or the company for their housing when they retire?

Do you have an equitable profit-sharing plan so that all may share equitably with the shareholders when the profit plan is met or exceeded?

19. Gifts and Donations

Advice

Encourage a spirit of generosity in your company and

set aside a portion of profits for charitable purposes.

In certain situations, a gift may be an acceptable act of appreciation; however, always be careful since the line of demarcation may be faint between a gift and a bribe; and the eyes of different beholders will see it as their perception wishes. If the company contributes to a political party or advocacy group, keep it legal and be open about it in your accounting records. In these sensitive areas, before you mail the check or send the gift, ask yourself the question: *"If this payment is reported on page one of tomorrow's main newspaper, will we be proud or embarrassed?"*

Queries

Do you set aside some money for charitable purposes each year?

Do you give your employees the opportunity to be stakeholders in how this should be allocated?

Do you encourage your staff to give to charities personally and do you provide procedures and mechanisms such as matching grants to help them to do so?

If you give gifts, do you do so without expectation of any return favors?

Are you sure that the recipient is not being put under an obligation?

If a business contact entertains you, do you pick up the tab at least half the time?

Do you make sure company entertaining does not conflict with a person's family and faith values?

Do you have a policy concerning the acceptance of gifts? Is it written, openly known, well understood, and followed at all levels of the company?

Remember, when dealing in this challenging area, the funds you are handling are not your personal assets; they are funds earned from an investment entrusted to you by your shareholders and lenders.

WORKING WITH PEOPLE

Consider that in business relationships, especially the workplace, we are yoked to one another in both a spiritual and practical journey. Be mindful that during the working week, we spend half or more of our waking hours in those workplaces. An integral and core value in many of the world's faiths is the admonition of the Golden Rule: *"Do unto others as you would have done unto you."*

Therefore, treat other people in the way you want to be treated. Remember that people have different values and that you might be dealing with people from a culture that is different from yours. Remember that people at all levels may at different times be angry, hurt, distracted, and hard to get along with, and as a result make mistakes or do things that are hurtful; be patient and be constructive in working to change their attitude. It is a proven fact that a soft answer does turn away wrath!

There will be times when an employee's competencies fail to match job requirements; when that occurs, face it, and with understanding and kindness, get them placed adequately, either in your company or another, with minimum cost, if any, to the employee. Use outplacement services if that will help ease the transition.

20. Responsibility of Employers to Employees

Advice

While much of Quaker thinking and practice of better ways to treat people in the workplace was developed during the early twentieth century, it is now generally accepted as normal practice. Early Quaker-owned businesses took the lead in reducing working hours, providing health and sickness benefits, pensions, life insurance and, in some cases, affordable housing.

Owners and managers do well to remember that while key physical assets of the company are annually tested, assessed, and certified by the external auditors, your human assets are not. Yet the human assets are equally or even more valuable to the company's success.

A key responsibility of business is to keep open the windows of opportunity. Management at all levels has a responsibility to bring out the best in people, encourage the growth of the whole person, and look out for the well-being of their employees.

If or when disputes occur, deal with them promptly; disputes do not improve with age. If you cannot see the best solution to the problem, get help, and quickly. Do not let disputes fester!

A clear dispute-resolution procedure must be known, understood, and accepted by all.

Queries

Are people proud to work for your company?

Do your employees see it as a good place to work?

Is the workplace safe, healthy, cheerful and congenial?

Do you treat your employees in the same way that you would like to be treated?

Do you have fair and understandable personnel policies that are administered equitably and consistently?

Do you have a regular program of performance and merit reviews, and do you adhere to that schedule?

When used, do you give volunteers the same care, consideration, and recognition as employees?

Do you provide flexible work schedules to allow for family commitments?

Do you provide such development opportunities for your employees in order that they can progress either in your business or another when an opportunity arises?

Do you support your staff and provide fair references when they decide to leave your employment?

When you have to terminate an employee, for whatever reason, do you act with fairness and kindness?

In a case of downsizing to meet changing business conditions, do you compensate your employee for all or part of the time it will take them to find another job?

Are you sensitive to conflict? Do you take prompt steps to prevent and resolve unnecessary disputes?

Do you have ways to detect disputes and deal with them before they become disruptive?

Do you have a clear grievance procedure that emphasizes mediation or arbitration?

21. Responsibility of Employees to Employers

Advice

Your employer is providing you and your family with a livelihood. Therefore, recognize that in return you are expected to earn your keep. Whatever your position, make sure that you take your full share of responsibility to make the company a success.

The workplace provides many facilities, opportunities and distractions; these may include telephones, e-mail, photocopiers, internet access, and so on. Make sure these are used for the furtherance of the business. Use of these for private convenience, entertainment or gain should be kept to a minimum, if at all. Remember that going beyond reasonable use is a betrayal of your employer's trust and is in fact theft.

Queries

Do you give a full day's work for your wage, salary or commission?

Do you avoid wasting your employer's, client's or customers' time?

Do you spend unnecessary time socializing on the job?

Do you speak up and tell your employer when you see problems or difficulties ahead?

Do you ask for permission to use company facilities for your own purposes?

Do you treat your employer and assets employed in the same way in which you would wish to be treated?

Do you disparage your company to others outside the workplace?

Are you pleasant, courteous, helpful and supportive to customers, suppliers and other employees?

Are you careful not to indulge in practices such as gossip, repeating rumors, or playing political games that are counterproductive to high morale and undermine team spirit?

22. Customers

Advice

Treat your customers with respect. Strive always for a win-win outcome in all customer-related matters. A satisfied customer is one who never walks away feeling aggrieved or mistreated.

Marketplace wisdom says the customer is always right; however, it is not always so. Always reserve the right to decline business from a customer who does not respect your rights as a supplier.

Be careful not to reveal information learned from one customer to another. To do so is a breach of trust and a very fast way to lose at least two, and possibly more valuable customers when your breach of good faith becomes known.

All businesses receive complaints from customers, some justifiable, and some not. Handle all complaints promptly and with fairness and equity, to maintain your reputation as a trusted quality supplier.

If and when you find a customer taking advantage of your "complaints and returns" policy in order to reduce their costs, confront the situation promptly with firmness and resolution. Be prepared to discard such a customer rather than being "nickeled-and-dimed to death." Commercial relationships, in which either party seeks to chisel the other, will be corrosive over time.

Queries

Do you treat your customers with appreciation and respect?

When serving multiple customers who may be competitors in the same business sector and industry, do you take all necessary precautions to be sure proprietary information of one, available to you as their trusted supplier, does not leak to their competitor(s)?

Are you candid and accurate in your assurances to them that their proprietary information that you possess is secure?

When you will miss a promised delivery date, do you tell your customer as soon as possible for their planning purposes, or do you wait until you are delinquent on delivery and they complain? Do you do all you can to minimize the problem for your customer, even at added costs to your business?

Is your final invoice compatible with your quote, or is it padded with extras?

Are you prepared to reject business from customers with a market reputation for squeezing their suppliers unethically?

Do you listen to customer complaints carefully and promptly correct the problem?

Do you replace faulty products or services quickly? Do you have a uniform and fair returns/rejection policy and procedure? Are your practices equally fair to both large and small customers?

Do you take all reasonable steps to deal with and rectify customer complaints as quickly as possible and make sure the causes are corrected internally in your company?

23. Suppliers

Advice

Treat the relationship with your suppliers in the same spirit and attitude as with your customer relationships. Reliable suppliers earn the same right to be respected as your customers. Remember, in times of critical shortages, suppliers can be more important than customers.

Reliable suppliers are very important to your business success, and they could become customers some time in the future.

Queries

Do you treat all suppliers with the respect they deserve?

If you have strong purchasing leverage, do you squeeze your suppliers unconscionably?

When you either end or scale down a long-standing relationship with a supplier, do you give them enough notice to adjust their business?

When a supplier provides credit terms, they are in fact partially financing your revenue cycle; do you treat that privilege with the respect it deserves and not stretch it out deliberately to the slow-pay category?

Do you strive to achieve lasting relationships of mutual trust with your suppliers? Do you treat their sales representatives courteously and use their time to mutual advantage?

Do you have contracts with key suppliers - for their protection as well as for your own?

Do you give your suppliers prompt, clear and helpful feedback when their goods or services are not up to the standard that you ordered?

24. Competitors

Advice

Respect your competitors. Making disrespectful comments about a competitor in the marketplace says more about you than about them.

Remember that you and your competitors set the reputation of your industry.

Within the spirit and intent of both state and federal laws, consider working jointly with your competitors within trade and industry groups, to provide new or better products or services to the market.

If at any time while talking with competitors either in or out of a trade or industry meeting and the conversation turns to illegal discussions on market sharing, adequacy of prices, profit margin improvement and similar topics, leave immediately and report the matter promptly to your management. Be sure to memorialize the incident in both your company and personal files. Avoid any appearance of unethical discussions at any time.

Queries

Do you avoid maligning or gossiping about your competitors?

Do you desist from industrial espionage?

If confidential information concerning a competitor is made available to you, do you refrain from exploiting such information or making inappropriate use of it?

Do you take all reasonable and prudent measures to protect your business, its intellectual and proprietary properties, and its employees, from industrial espionage, hackers, and malicious cyber attacks?

Are you willing to refer a customer to a competitor when you cannot provide what the customer needs?

Do you try to entice customers away from competitors by unethical means?

Do you totally avoid market sharing and price-fixing arrangements?

Do all of your employees understand your policy about competitors, and do they also understand that if they violate that policy they risk termination? Do employees understand that the legal risk they are undertaking is theirs alone and not the company's? In addition, do they understand that should they violate any antitrust laws, there is no obligation of the company to defend them for such violations?

25. Caring for Oneself

Advice

In business, as in life's other activities, common sense requires that each person takes good care of themselves in all dimensions of their physical, mental, and spiritual health.

Develop and keep to work patterns, personal habits, and a life style that controls the stress and pressures in your life. Exercise self-discipline to handle both your work, rest and recreation patterns effectively, so living a balanced and full life for both your benefit and your family's.

Queries

Do you take sufficient rest and vacation in order that your health, both physical and mental, is refreshed and keeps you effective both as a person and as a manager?

Do you test and make sure that you know both your personal and your management's capacities, in order that you set realistic and achievable objectives for both yourself and the management team?

Do you qualify and quantify business challenges and problems, such that you avoid unnecessary anxieties and possibly poor decisions as a result?

Do you seek counsel from experienced people of proven business wisdom and acumen both inside and outside your business when in need or when contemplating new directions?

Do you think carefully of the timing of when to hand over the reins to others, to sell, or to retire? If you decide to sell, are you prepared to invest the time and effort to be sure that the buyer is a company you would want to work for, even if they are not the high bidder for your company?

Do you allow others to participate fully in the work and responsibility of your business so that neither you nor they are overburdened or overstressed?

Are you generous in praise for others who do a good job?

Are you open to sharing your burdens as well as your joys with others?

THE COMMUNITY

The whole business and industrial community today tends to be an international network of people and organizations. Any business is involved in the community at many levels. First of all, companies must build a thriving community both within their organization and their surrounding environs. At another level, a company is involved in a broader community that includes suppliers, customers, bankers, governments, and others. Increasingly, at yet another level, companies, regardless of size, may well be involved in the global economy. The world of business is now, as it has been for centuries, a dynamic case study of the interdependence of diverse countries, races, creeds, business practices using varying standards of ethics and morality, languages, currencies, and senses of timeliness in task completions. The task for managers is to work through this maze without getting a terminal case of management vertigo.

26. Local Community

Advice

The community in which you operate consists of homes, other businesses, schools, shops, social, recreational, and other services. Although it is easier to be recognized for what you do in a small community, in a large city the same concern for the community supporting your people and company also applies.

Try to manage your business affairs to be an asset to your communities, and not a liability.

If asked to support a local activity that benefits your people as well as others, find a way to just do it!

Queries

Are you actively involved in working for the improvement of the community in which you and your company operate?

How does your reputation, and your company's reputation, stand locally?

Do you unreasonably take advantage of the community to improve your profits at their expense?

27. Government

Advice

Wisely and intelligently managed businesses operate within both the spirit and intent of the law: local, national, and international. Monitoring and understanding the impact of legislation can be difficult, time consuming, and sometimes very frustrating. Nonetheless, that critical job has to be done and done well. For the most part, business laws do not adversely affect businesses that are managed prudently and ethically. Always remember that ignorance of the law is not exculpatory if the law is broken.

If you discover you are operating outside the law, correct the situation as speedily as possible, with advice as necessary from legal counsel. There is no more costly dilution of the constructive use of management's time and efforts than being involved in a lawsuit; the same can be said for the unnecessary use of shareholder funds for the legal costs.

Queries

In all your business affairs, do you keep within the law?

Do you make sure that you are regularly informed about the laws and regulations that apply to your business?

Do you respect and comply with the spirit and intent of these laws and regulations?

Do you join with others to take positive steps to change those laws and regulations that you believe are unjust, immoral, or counterproductive to good business?

28. Labor Unions

Advice

Remember that it is the task of union leaders to constructively negotiate for, and look after, the best interests of their members, leading inevitably to pressing for job security, good working conditions, and optimal rates of pay. In all of your dealings with unions, maintain a positive and sincere attitude of mutual respect and trust such that both of you will do your best to make your organization successful. The objective of negotiations is to achieve a positive outcome for all parties.

Do not disparage the role of unions and their leaders either in public or in private. Remember that you are *appointed* to your management position; union leaders are *elected* by their membership. This means that union leaders may act and react in a political way at times, and you should recognize that and handle it with understanding and tolerance. This does not mean, however, that you have to "give away the store" either.

Queries

Do you live up to the spirit and intent of your collective bargaining agreement with the union?

Do you keep promises that you make to unions and their leaders? Is your word your bond?

Do you ask more from unions than you would be prepared to give if you were in their position?

Are your management policies and practices designed to avoid unnecessary conflict and confrontation with unions?

Do you view the employer, the employees, and the union leaders, as a yoked team, each of whom shares a key role in making the business very successful?

29. Pressure Groups

Advice

There well may be times when a product or service, a price, or a perceived lack of competition may be seen by a vocal minority to be wrong. If you are the company affected, keep calm, and do not ignore the situation. Consider carefully what has been said, what is factual and what is not, and what, if anything, you should or can do about it. If the company is in the wrong, admit it, do your "mea culpa," and get on with the company's business, and don't waste shareholders' moneys on public relations extravaganzas.

Remember, in emotionally charged situations, those who lose their temper will inevitably lose the argument and will certainly lose respect.

Queries

If your business is the focus of a pressure group, do you take time to meet with them, try to understand their complaint, explain your position, and try to come to some amicable solution?

When appropriate, and in the best interests of your investors and employees, do you join with others to work for a more ethical business world?

Do you make sure that any advocacy groups to which you or your company may belong are ethically and morally based?

UNETHICAL BUSINESS PRACTICES

Many people in business have, at one time or another, been confronted with unethical business practices. These practices, when publicized in the media, inevitably serve to give business a bad reputation. How a board, management and employees respond to these situations will involve making difficult decisions, even to the point of "whistle-blowing" as a last resort.

30. Gambling and Speculation

Advice

Gambling is a zero-sum-minus game, since what one party loses the other party wins, minus the "house skim." The house never loses.

When business managers invest in exceptionally risky ventures with the hope of an exorbitant future return, that is speculation!

Unrealistic confidence and optimism, or an addiction to the excitement of dealings in futures markets, can lead to losses of shareholder assets and ultimately to financial disaster. In a business situation, speculation will not only put company assets at risk, but also your employees' job security.

Queries

Do you invest or otherwise use company funds for speculative purposes or in a business gamble?

Do you entertain business customers at casinos or similar venues that pander to gamblers?

If your company requires commodities that are traded on a commodity exchange, do you speculate on those commodities or maintain a prudently hedged position?

31. Corrupt Practices

Advice

By whatever name, bribes, come-sure, grease, baksheesh, graft, squeeze, payoffs, foreign political contributions, kickbacks, and other payment practices of a similar nature that we would consider both illegal and corrupt are commonly accepted in some industries and cultures. Make sure that your employees are aware of the Foreign Corrupt Practices Act and alert to all kinds of practices that are not acceptable.

Queries

Do you have a clear written policy statement covering business conduct that all employees affirm they understand and then sign?

Do you avoid all forms of bribery and corruption, both within your own business and in your dealings with business partners?

When you work in international markets and cultures where some form of bribery and high sales commissions are both expected and a way of life, do you try to find ways of doing business that more closely express your own ethical standards?

Do you discourage and correct inappropriate working and management practices in your workplaces? Do you speak out against corrupt practices that you discover?

32. Whistle Blowing

Advice

Before blowing the whistle on a person, an organization, or on a particular business practice, consider carefully the possible consequences of your actions. Your primary role, if any, is to be a witness to the truth, the whole truth, and nothing but the truth. Be sure that you fully and completely comprehend and understand the reasons for the alleged practice and that your evidence really is evidence and will withstand public and legal review in the cold gray dawns in the days following your disclosure.

Make sure that your own motives will withstand the full

heat and light of public scrutiny. Act promptly and prudently as soon as you are sure of the actions you intend to follow. Whenever possible, seek advice, wise counsel, and guidance from others of proven business wisdom and acumen. When possible, work through an agency so as to remove irrelevant and counterproductive emotion and personality from the situation and to allow truth and facts to prevail. Be emotionally and also intellectually prepared for the backlash that will inevitably follow. Always be sure of your motives in such an action, which will undoubtedly be subject to serious scrutiny before the matter is resolved.

Queries

Is the action you contemplate likely to lead to a change for the better? If not, what is your motivation? Is there a better or less confrontational way of dealing with the situation?

Have you and your family considered that your action might cost you your job and will affect, for better or worse, your personal life, your professional and business reputation, and your career?

Have you used independent and wise counsel before proceeding? In your company's culture, do all employees, from top to bottom in the company, have the mutual trust and confidence to deal with unethical and improper business practices, either inside or outside the organization?

Do you have a procedure in place such that any employee can, if necessary, blow the whistle to an ombudsperson without being penalized?

VISION, PRACTICE & PRAGMATISM

Lofty visions, ideals, principles and aims on their own are not enough; they need to be catalyzed into action daily in both our personal and business lives. The means are as important as the ends we seek to achieve.

Contrary to wishful thinking, public relations imaging, and self-delusion, none of us can claim to be perfect. Our methods and practices must take account of our own limitations and capacity for mistakes as well as the failures and frailties of others.

Balancing discipline, especially self-discipline, with freedom, exploration, and pragmatism, is important for us to grow spiritually and realize our business vision and goals. Above all, do not forget to take your humility pills daily! Remember too that failure will always occur to those whose power of persuasion is so great they cannot withstand themselves.

33. Leadership and Decision Making

Advice

In each business situation someone needs to take the initiative to lead the way forward and to motivate the team to continuing realizations of the common vision.

From time to time we are all called upon to lead; when it is your turn, do so with courage, sensitivity, and hard-headed drive.

In business situations, it is important to share and discuss your views with others, in order to fix the optimal course of action for the group or the company. Consider all the stakeholders affected, not just the immediate players. Planning is a three-step process. First, assess your current position. Second, determine the plan. And third, successfully execute the plan! It is necessary both to make a decision and to act. Remember the necessity for contingency planning to take care of the situations when the "what if?" situations you hoped would not happen do happen! Keep in mind Murphy's Law, viz., "If anything bad can happen, it usually will!" Remember too, the advice of an Eastern wise man who said: "He who plans for the future by the crystal ball should learn to eat ground glass."

Queries

Are you both competent and prepared to take responsibility for making decisions?

Do you consult with those affected and seek out best thinking, strategies and tactics?

Do you carefully consider the "what ifs" and develop appropriate contingency plans?

Do you avoid protracted and thus paralyzing indecision?

Are you open to the advice and guidance of others for whom and with whom you work?

When a decision has to be made, do you explain its ramifications to those affected, so that they understand the goal and the part that they have in its realization? If the decision is not the one you wanted to see, do you still give it your best effort and not undercut it in public or private conversations?

34. Management

Advice

One hallmark of good management is the successful combination of scarce resources with good planning, organization, and facilities to serve end markets of value to society. This means giving people a productive framework in which to work and enabling them to do a good job in the face of limitations.

Good management builds and maintains a cohesive spirit of teamwork, bringing out the best in people and enhancing job satisfaction and goal attainment.

Determine the leverage factors which make your workplaces happy and productive. Then set about to create and implement them.

When the time comes for you to move on, be sure the team you leave behind is better than the one you inherited.

Queries

Do you respect your employees?

Do you adopt combined attitudes of respect and trust to all, even though in some cases it may not be reciprocated?

Do you exemplify a positive role model which could be a case study for others to see the best in management practice?

Does your managerial competence and behavior earn their respect? Do you avoid corrosive management blame-games and 'put-downs'?

Do you communicate your plans, concerns, and expectations clearly, appropriately, and in a timely manner?

Do you delegate?

Do you try to make each person's job more satisfying by giving them as much responsibility as they can manage with commensurate authority?

If you supervise others, do you remember that this is your opportunity to help them contribute their best? Are you both a builder as well as a user of human assets?

Do you give constructive performance feedback of both praise and correction, in such a way that there is no loss of face when that occurs?

Are you careful to praise and reward others for their efforts and achievements?

Do you pass on compliments from your customers? If someone makes a mistake, do you consider how you can help the person concerned to learn from that experience?

Do you avoid humiliating employees either in public or in private?

Are you sensitive that everyone has their own family and problems and may, from time to time, need your understanding and support?

When difficult human relations problems arise, do you remember that even those who are hostile or who abuse our trust are entitled to be treated fairly and legally? Are you careful to keep an objective record of events?

35. Monitoring, Feedback Loops, and Audits

Advice

Every well-managed and successful business can be so and remain so, only by utilizing feedback information systems to monitor the company's performance against plan. This has to be done on a dynamic basis rather than using historical accounting information which at best is always "past tense." Such information tells you only what has happened, and is not future-looking to what can optimally be the best end result. A good feedback system will alert you to future problems, enabling you to address potential problems quickly and proactively.

Monitoring and feedback information loops are critical as well for product and service quality control, and when practiced constructively, result in continuous improvement in performance.

These activities should take place in an open and constructive way.

Those people responsible for monitoring should be appropriately qualified and respect both the rights of individuals and the company's reputation as a quality supplier and a good place to work.

Queries

Does your business have efficient systems for monitoring, auditing, and quality assurance?

Do you make sure that all engaged in monitoring functions are competent and qualified for their tasks?

Do you ensure that the results of your monitoring and performance measurement are fed back to the right people constructively and sensitively?

Do you use monitoring and feedback to improve people's quality of life at work as well as to improve the company's performance?

36. Confidentiality

Advice

All that is personal about an individual, including that person's feelings and even your observations and assessment of that person is confidential. Treat anything in a one-to-one meeting as confidential, unless it is clearly and mutually understood to be for public consumption.

Similarly, always treat discussions about an individual in confidence. Remember, in business, under civil rights and employment laws, employees are entitled to know what has been written or even said about them in a meeting, and have access to any and all information in their personnel records in the company's files.

Comply with both the spirit and the intent of legislation protecting the privacy of others.

Queries

Can people confide in you, with no reservations? Do you treat all information entrusted to you with discretion, integrity, and responsibility?

Are you careful to avoid the use of management tools and techniques that either limit or betray the trust, confidence, or privacy of others, and lead to a sense of mistrust if and when brought out to the light of full public scrutiny?

Are you careful not to take proprietary information from one customer or supplier and give that to another for your commercial advantage?

Are you careful not to use or distribute confidential information?

If you received confidential material belonging to a competitor, what do you do with it?

37. Intellectual Property

Advice

The ownership, use, and protection of intellectual property have become increasingly important with the broadening scope of cyber business. Make absolutely sure that your company's intellectual properties are completely protected; and, if and when necessary, legally defended.

In like vein, respect the intellectual property rights of others, competitors, customers, suppliers, and in the public domain at large. Remember also that the unlicensed use of another party's intellectual property without permission and/or payment is both unethical and illegal. With increasing global competition, the protection of your intellectual property entails both domestic and international tasks.

Queries

Do you implement a strict policy that your company or its employees do not infringe the copyrights, patents, trademarks, proprietary know-how or other intellectual property rights of others?

Do you acknowledge all sources of your work product, both within and outside your company?

When you copy or use artwork, do you check to find out who owns the copyright?

Do you ask for permission to use the material? Do you make sure that the changes you make are acceptable to the owner?

Are you careful about copies made for private study?

Do you use computer software for which you have not paid?

Do you use all necessary legal means at your disposal to register and protect your own intellectual property?

If you or your company invents or develops a product, process or service which could be, or perhaps ought to be, in the public domain, how do you decide what fee, if any, to charge for its use? What the market will bear?

If you do not properly protect your property rights from domestic and/or foreign piracy, how do you propose to stop unethical supplier(s) from usurping your rights and skimming the markets for your products?

ADVICES FROM AN AMERICAN QUAKER BUSINESSMAN

One of the American editors/authors of this text is a Quaker whose career was spent in the American steel industry. He rose from trainee to the top position of a Fortune 500 company in that industry as chairman, president and chief executive. His principles of management, which he attributes in part to the early writings of the Scots businessman David Ogilvy, are set out below as a reference text. It is his view that similar principles guided the Quaker businessmen who built enterprises such as Barclays and Lloyds Banks, Price Waterhouse, companies serving the consumer markets like Rowntree, Cadbury, Carr, Huntley and Palmers, Reckitt and Coleman in chemicals, and Coalbrookdale in iron and steel, to name only a few. His operating principles are set out below.

General

The company is dedicated to these key purposes:

- To maintain high ethical standards.

- To serve our customers more effectively than our competitors do.

- To earn an increased profit every year.

- To manage the company with a healthy sense of competitive urgency.

- To keep our products and services the best in the industry.

- To make the company an exciting place to work.

- To earn the respect of the community.

Profitability

Increased sales are not synonymous with increased profit; we pursue profit, not sales. The main ways we can increase profits are the following. Increase income from present customers. Get new customers. Get rid of freeloaders from our customer books without delay. Get rid of boondoggles, and obsolete products and services quickly.

Avoid duplication of functions - two people doing what one can and should do is counterproductive and demoralizing. Increase productivity. Put idle capital to work. Keep the barnacles scraped off the ship's hull; it's your job and do it!

Morale

Internal politics in a company are a waste of time and effort better devoted to building the company; work with firmness to eliminate them. Some suggestions are:

- Be fair, open and honest in your own actions; unfairness, dishonesty, and cronyism at the top will demoralize a company in time.

- Do not hire relatives and friends.

- Firmly encourage incurable office-politicians to seek a career path in a venue other than your company.

- Lower the boom on paper, fax, or electronic warfare; encourage people to settle differences face-to-face.

- Discourage secrecy.

- Discourage managerial poaching in other managers' preserves.

- Resolve sibling rivalries in management, and promptly!

- Encourage upward and lateral communication; seek people's advice and listen to it; be candid with them, and encourage reciprocal candor.

- Build a sense of pride in the company and make the company a stimulating place to work. Exhibit a sense of humor; grimness achieves zero. Encourage change; stagnation is the first step down the slippery slope of mediocrity. Don't summon people to your office, see them in their workplace; they'll be more at ease and communicate better.

- Maintain a can-do attitude in your approach to challenges, and offer encouragement to pessimists who may spread gloom, always seeing the glass as half empty. Counsel them to see the glass as half full, and if they cannot make this adjustment, counsel them out.

If you expect your team to be hard working, set the example yourself.

Respect

One of the priceless assets of the company is respect: of our customers, suppliers, employees, competitors, and communities. As with any asset of value, it's our job to earn and keep that respect continually. Suggestions are:

- Management must be made up of the kind of men and women who command respect; no phonies, cronies, legacies, or zeros.

- Always be honest and open with our customers; no double-talk or weaseling excuses when we goof up on delivery, quality, or service.

- If we do a good job for our customers, it becomes known in the marketplace, and we will earn its respect.

- Treat our employees and all with whom we deal with decency, courtesy and consideration and they will speak well of us. When that happens, the multiplier effect of good repute is remarkable, and respect follows.

- Do your part; pull your weight as a good citizen.

Remember the Golden Rule: "Always treat others as you would like them to treat you; that is the Law and the prophets." (Matthew 7:12 and Luke 6:31)

Hiring

Always hire the best you can; if you have the good luck to find people better than you are, hire them quickly. Remember, you can't be promoted unless you have a person ready to fill your shoes either as good or better than yourself. If you create and maintain an exciting and stimulating workplace, you'll have no trouble recruiting and holding good people. By your example set, do not let prejudice in any way creep into your hiring practices; it's illegal, immoral and unethical, and as a practice one we would abhor if applied to us!

Teamwork

Several suggestions:

- Have clear-cut divisions of responsibility.

- Discourage poaching in other managers' preserves.

- Practice tolerance, and a sense of humor, especially when the joke is on you.

- Live and let live; nobody is perfect.

"Why beholdest thou the mote in thy brother's eye, and not considerest the beam in thine own eye?" (Matthew 7:3-5 and Luke 6:41-42)

Talent

The most important asset we have in the company is our people; more so than our plants and facilities. The care and nurture of our people is a management task we must never shirk. It is important to spot women and men of talent and move them up the management ladder as fast as they can handle increased responsibility and as opportunities occur. There are characteristics that mark a rising star, and some are: they have a healthy ambition and drive; they work hard and enjoy their work; they do not complete their tasks at the expense of others; they have a good mind and intellect and use both; they are team players, and know and respect that others are smart too; and they are builders of human assets, not "users" of people.

Failure to recognize, develop, and promote these people (especially the young ones) will mean losing them; management talent is mobile, and human resource headhunters see the management pool of successful companies as the ideal place for recruiting.

Summary

Management has the key responsibility for the success and the security of the company and its assets, human, physical and financial. It must see to it that the company remains on the cutting edge of its markets, indeed, be the market leader. Remember, you in management are always managing change, and if your speed in making change as demanded by the market, and thus needed within your organization, is not at a faster rate of change than both the market and your competition, you'll be left behind, period! The corporate burying grounds have many headstones of companies whose managements either could not or would not see, then face up to and appropriately react to the changes demanded by the market and thus soon became terminal. Who suffered? The shareholders, employees, suppliers, customers, and communities; all of whom placed their trust in their management, who were in fact, the trustees for those "trusters."

QUAKER DECISION-MAKING METHODS

The Quaker method of conducting meetings for business and arriving at decisions is quite different from the way most businesses handle decision-making.

First, our business meetings carry the expectation that God's guidance can be discerned if we truly listen together. The primary objective is to seek unity in decisions: to find a way forward that is acceptable to all present. This is not easy to do, especially when the issue is a controversial one, or when there are strongly held opposing views. The outcome is not necessarily one with which everyone agrees, but one that all present can accept and fully support, in the knowledge that their views have been heard and considered. We must recognize that a minority view may continue to exist.

There are some Quaker ways of conducting meetings which others might find useful.

The Use of Silence

Silence itself has no magic. It may be just sheer emptiness or absence of sound. However, the effective use of silence in business meetings can create a powerful atmosphere for the reception of inspiration and guidance.

Quaker meetings for business always begin and end with silent worship. At the beginning, the silence makes a break with what has gone before. It also gives time to focus on the task at hand and to concentrate on playing your part in discerning the way forward. Silence at the end helps to provide a peaceful closure. Some of us have found that in tense or emotionally charged situations, a short period of silence can have a calming effect. When discussions become heated, the call for a few minutes' silence to reflect on the matter under consideration can often help.

Conduct of Business Meetings

An appointed clerk chairs every meeting for business. The clerk's task is not just to keep the meeting going according to the agenda, or to record the proceedings in minutes that will be disseminated afterwards. The clerk's primary role is to be able to gauge the sense of the meeting, and to bring minds together so that an acceptable way forward can be agreed. When the way forward has been found, the clerk drafts a minute recording the decision, which is read back and an acceptable way forward is achieved. With true unity, respect for minority opinions will enable those who held minority views to join in supporting the decision. This method takes patience and insight, but it has advantages. It enables all opinions to be heard so that everyone should be comfortable with the outcome. It creates clarity because the minute has been agreed at the time, whilst the issues are fresh in people's minds. This reduces subsequent differences of opinion and revisions to minutes.

Meeting for Clearness

This is a special form of meeting to help a person or group of people make a difficult decision, or to seek guidance at times of change, tension, disagreement, or difficulty. A small number of people are appointed for their special knowledge or experience to help those present become clear about possible options and ways forward. A relaxed atmosphere of trust is important, and confidentiality must be maintained within the group.

A facilitator may be chosen to assist in clarifying the questions. This is a time for listening with undivided attention.

The Quakers and Business Group

The British Quakers and Business Group was founded in 1998 by Quakers who were concerned about the growing attitude of ethically minded people that it is somehow wrong to work in any organization that strives to make a profit. This negative view may not be confined to Quakers. We recognize that business is not without its faults. This book offers suggestions to operate in ways that will help to modify and eventually eliminate those practices that give business a bad name.

Looking inward, we believe that there is much that religious groups, including the Religious Society of Friends and other faith-based organizations, can both learn from and contribute to the business world.

Reference Texts

The Quakers, Money and Morals, by Professor James Walvin, Professor of History, York University, United Kingdom. Published by John Murray Publishers Ltd., London, 1997. An excellent history of Quakers in U.K. business, spanning several centuries up to modern times.

On Moral Business, Published in 1995 by Wm. B. Eerdmans Publishing Co., Grand Rapids, Michigan. A valuable text edited by Max L. Stackhouse, Dennis P. McCann and Shirley J. Roels with Preston N. Williams. A comprehensive compilation of nearly one hundred papers covering the religious, ethical, and moral undergirding of business.

About the Editor

Phillip Hartley Smith was born in Sydney, Australia, on January 26, 1927, the youngest of Captain and Mrs. Norman E. Smith's five children. Following service in the Australian Forces during World War II, he majored in Mining and Metallurgy at the University of Sydney, was a Nuffield Scholar, and a member of Wesley College. He graduated with first class honors and head of his class in 1950.

Smith came to the United States in 1950 as a Fulbright Scholar to study Metallurgy and Industrial Management at the Massachusetts Institute of Technology. Graduating in 1952, with a terminal engineering degree in metallurgy, and a minor from the Sloan School, his thesis was on steelmaking, under Dr. John Chipman, a pioneer in steelmaking research.

Joining Inland Steel Company in Chicago as a metallurgical engineer, Smith gained operating experience in the blast furnace, rolling mills, quality control, and steelmaking departments at its Indiana Harbor Works. While at Inland, Smith and Professor John Elliott of M.I.T. were awarded the National Steelmaking Award for their outstanding technical paper by the American Institute of Mining and Metallurgical Engineers. Smith also published papers on blast furnace production, alloying of steel, and manufacture of free-machining steels, where he is a patentee. Recognized by the American Society of Metals and the American Institute of Mining and

Metallurgical Engineers for his contributions to metallurgy and materials science, he is past chairman of the Mechanical Working Committee of AIMME and was editor of its text on mechanical working of steel. He is a member of the M.I.T. Chapter of Sigma Xi, the national scientific research society.

In 1956 Smith moved on to LaSalle Steel Company, a privately owned manufacturer of specialty steels and hydraulic equipment. He was successively a research engineer, Director of Purchases, and Director of Purchasing and Planning. During that period he earned a Diploma in Industrial Relations at the University of Chicago. He became an American citizen in 1960.

Smith joined Copperweld Corporation at its steel plant in Warren, Ohio, as an assistant to the executive vice-president in October 1964. In 1966 he was elected Vice President of Development, 1967 Senior Vice-President, and President and Chief Executive Officer in December 1967. In 1973 he was elected Chairman of the Board. Copperweld grew substantially during the ten years of his leadership, becoming one of the most profitable companies in the industry. "Financial World" magazine named him one of the three outstanding chief executives in the steel and metal-working industries. M.I.T. has recognized him for his distinguished corporate leadership.

After ten years as Chief Executive, Smith resigned from Copperweld and subsequently joined the Bekaert

Group of Belgium to become the President of its North American operations. Bekaert N.V. is the world's largest maker of wire and wire products. Following three years of record earnings for the American subsidiary, Smith resigned in 1982 to form his own private consulting company, Smith Yuill & Co. Inc. The firm advises strategic planning and turnaround-workout situations for major banks, government bodies, and corporations in the U.S., Japan, Australia, New Zealand, and the Peoples Republic of China. Smith has advised the U.S. Government's Pension Benefit Guaranty Corporation on bankruptcy workout matters.

Smith was the publisher of the "American Economic Commentary." He holds patents in his field, has edited and written texts on management, and has published and lectured on management science and strategic planning. He has taught at Purdue University, been a guest lecturer at the business schools of M.I.T., Carnegie-Mellon, the University of Pittsburgh, Grove City College, Berea College, and Ashland College, and has lectured on management science and strategic planning to The Institute of Management Science. Smith was invited by the Chinese Government for a number of years to the Dalian University of Technology, in Manchuria, China, to lecture on various aspects of management disciplines from the chief executive's view with special emphasis on turnaround management, rebuilding, and growth management strategies, and served as Dean of Dalian's Senior Executive Program. He served on the Advisory Committee for the U.S. Commerce

Department's management development program in China, and he wrote a text on management for use at Dalian - "A Guide to Executives on the Way Up."

Included in the boards of business and public organizations on which he has served are: McGraw Edison, Pittsburgh National Bank, Second National Bank of Warren, Ohio, Imetal (France), Japan Alumoweld Co. (Japan), Seldon & Co. (Australia), Copperweld Corp., Bekaert Steel Wire Co., Presbyterian Ministers' Fund Life Insurance Co., American Iron & Steel Institute of which he is an Honorary Fellow, Kaiser Steel, Adience Corp., Weirton Steel Corporation, YMCA of Pittsburgh, Hospital Planning Association, Gordon Conwell Theological Seminary, Pittsburgh Theological Seminary, McClintock Associates (Australia), Bell of Pennsylvania, and Salem Corporation. Smith currently serves on the board of NASA's National Technology Transfer Center and I.D.I. Corporation.

Smith has had extensive experience on board audit committees, chairing those committees for Bell of Pennsylvania, P.M.F. Life Insurance, Weirton Steel, and Adience. He is a former trustee of Berea College, and of Grove City College, which awarded him an LLD in 1975, and has served as an adjunct professor of Grove City College. He is Vice Chairman of the Board of Wheeling Jesuit University, served as a trustee of the Presbyterian Foundation, and is past Chairman of the Pittsburgh M.I.T. Enterprise Forum. He has served on the Fox Chapel School Board, and is the past Chairman of Inroads Inc., a national organization established to assist minority students in business and engineering. In 1999 the University of Sydney awarded him the degree of Doctor of Engineering.

Smith is a member of The Pittsburgh Meeting of the Religious Society of Friends.

Mrs. Smith is the President of Mitech Laboratories Inc., and past President of the Girl Scouts of Southwestern Pennsylvania. She is an Honorary Associate of the World Association of Girl Guides and Girl Scouts, and she serves on the board of the Mars Home for Youth, the Investment Committee of the American Waldensian Society, and served on the Board of the Olave Baden Powell Society for nine years. She is an Elder and former Clerk of Session of the First Presbyterian Church of Pittsburgh, and serves on the Committee on Ministry of Pittsburgh Presbytery.